The Beer Drinker's Dream Diet

by Elwin W. Law

Winnstead Publishing
La Jolla, California 92038

© 1991 by Winnstead Publishing Co.
P.O. Box 874
La Jolla, CA 92038
Tel.: (619) 459-3612
ISBN 0-9631321-0-5
Printed in the United States of America

Dedicated to the 80 million beer
drinkers in this country and their mates.

A special appreciation to the national
organization of Beer Drinkers of America,
headquartered in Costa Mesa, California.
1 (800) 441-BEER

Author's Note

As with any diet, check with your physician before beginning *The Beer Drinker's Dream Diet*. However, I am certain he or she will agree that it's really too healthy to be turned down by anyone!

Acknowledgment

I am especially grateful to Dr. Susan Friedland for her editing, and for her medical footnotes throughout the book relating to the principles in *The Beer Drinker's Dream Diet*.

Elwin Law

Foreword

The laws of thermodynamics are inexorable and unyielding: If we consume more calories than we burn, weight is gained. If we consume less than we burn, weight is lost.

As we grow older, metabolism slows down, which simply means that we burn somewhat fewer calories than we did in our youth. If we continue to eat as we did in our youth, pounds creep on year by year.

Elwin Law, in his delightful book, *The Beer Drinker's Dream Diet*, hasn't repealed the laws of thermodynamics, but he has shown us how to deal with them in a balanced program of diet and exercise that makes no overpowering demands upon willpower. In fact, it doesn't really deny us any of the foods or beverages that make life truly worth living — *beer* included!

This is a simple program that you can use, not for a few weeks or a few months, but *forever*! It works! Try it — you'll like it!

Herb Boynton

How would you like to continue enjoying your beer as you do now and *still* lose 10 to 30 pounds within two to ten weeks?

Yes, you can— and in a totally healthy way!

How would you also like to get the same results even though you may not drink beer?

Please keep reading . . .

The Beer Drinker's Dream Diet — It Works!

I have no apologies to make — I *like* beer. I especially enjoy it after a hard game of tennis. I like the way it tastes and I like the mellow glow I feel after a few beers with friends. I absolutely love beer with my evening meal.

I first developed a real taste for the golden brew when I was stationed in Germany back in the 1960s. Germany has some of the finest beer in the world, a fact to which anyone who has been there would attest. (Remember the Oktoberfest in Munich?)

To be honest with you, dieting (what an unpleasant word) has never been important enough to me to make me give up my beer, even though up to very recently I was fifteen to twenty pounds overweight.

How many of us have heard over and over from well-meaning friends, spouses, and/or lovers, "If you would only give up beer, you would lose weight!" Well, not only did I not give up beer, I continued my enjoyment with gusto.

But I'll tell you what I DID do . . . For the first time ever, I combined some very special principles that allowed me to continue drinking as much beer as I wanted and at the same time achieve a fantastically healthy drop in weight — from 202 to 175 pounds, with a decrease in waist size from 38 to 32 inches — all in a matter of *ten short weeks*! And all through those weeks, I continued to enjoy my beer as I went merrily along losing weight.

One of the most important benefits of all was that I have *maintained* this weight loss with the greatest of ease, with only a 3- or 4-pound fluctuation.

To me, this was indeed a dream of a diet — one I'd never heard of or read about anywhere.

Thus, the title of this book, *The Beer Drinker's Dream Diet*. It's fun! It's effortless! And, most of all, IT WORKS!!

There are two points I want you to remember:

- NUMBER ONE: I *wanted* to lose weight. The *desire* was there to shed at least a portion of those excess 24 pounds. *But . . .*

- NUMBER TWO (and this was decidedly much stronger than Number 1): I had no intention of sacrificing anything in order to lose this weight, nor of depriving myself in the least — especially as far as beer was concerned!

In short, I wanted to have my beer and drink it too. And you know what? I found a very healthy way of doing it!

If *that's* not something special, and not something that everyone who buys a diet book is looking for, then I don't know what is.

What the "Dream Diet" Did for Me

- In approximately ten weeks, I *comfortably* went from 202 to 175 pounds while maintaining maximum strength.

- In the same period of time, I went from a 38-inch waist to a 32-inch waist.

- My stamina and energy level increased substantially: (I truly can't remember when I've felt better!)

- My blood pressure dropped.

- This weight loss was one of the EASIEST things I've ever done in relation to the results achieved.

- My personal physician was absolutely delighted at my last checkup.

- There was a slight decrease in my bank account due to major tailoring requirements!

Imagine . . .

C lose your eyes for a moment and imagine how you would feel if you could eat three meals a day — basically foods of your own choice — and still lose anywhere from 10 to 30 pounds in two to ten weeks.

- Imagine eating and drinking anything you want every evening — including beer — and *still* losing that much weight.

- Imagine the clothes you presently have hanging on you like a sack, in dire need of immediate alteration to fit your new trim body. A body which people have openly started to admire regardless of your age.

- Sense for a moment the new feeling you have about yourself as people comment on how good you look, and having this

new image confirmed daily by your re-
flection in the mirror.

- Listen for a moment to your doctor telling you that you are in the best physical
  shape you've been in for years, that your
  blood pressure is down, and that some of
  those aches and pains that come with
  being overweight have either disappeared
  or decreased significantly.

  Imagine, once you have lost the desired
  weight, being able to *keep* it off, fluctuat-
  ing only two to four pounds.

- Feel your new strength and energy puls-
  ing through your body, no longer
  weighted down and depleted by those
  excess pounds. It's much like having
  gotten rid of a 20-pound bowling ball
  you've been carrying everywhere with
  you.

Feel the surge of vitality in everything you do. Enjoy the sensuous feeling of being close to someone special, as if the years had melted away back to the time you were your most exciting and sexiest self.

- Imagine that you could accomplish this 10- to 30-pound weight loss, along with all its other benefits, with only fifteen to twenty minutes of fun exercise a day — fitting it into your own schedule and doing it at your own pace, in the privacy of your own home if you choose.

- And most importantly, imagine accomplishing all this and never feeling DEPRIVED for a moment! No feeling of sacrifice, hunger pangs, or depression.

Instead, imagine a wonderful feeling of accomplishment, a glorious and healthy momentum that perpetuates itself. Imagine *you* being in control, and adding ingredients to your program to suit you personally.

What is so special about *The Beer Drinker's Dream Diet* is that no weight-loss program anywhere is *EASIER*. I have taken six basic principles and, for the first time, combined them in a special way that produces magnificent results — these same results you have just imagined.

Whoever heard of eating three meals a day, drinking whatever you like, and still losing substantial weight with no feeling of sacrifice?

The beauty of this book is the incredible *ease* by which you can accomplish all this, *including* a major improvement in health. Let's see what several people had to say about *The Beer Drinker's Dream Diet*:

H. Clay Alexander, M.D.

and Associates, P.A.

9335 Garland Road

Dallas, Texas 75218

Elwin Law
7760 Fay Avenue
Suite Q
La Jolla, CA 92037

Dear Elwin,

Reading *The Beer Drinker's Dream Diet* was a joy. At last someone has really gotten down to the basics of how to lose weight. Your diet doesn't cost anything except the price of your book! It is absolutely painless, as you are eating the foods you like, and there should be none of the complications that can be associated with most of the expensive "fancy" diets on the market today. And . . . it works just as well for non-beer drinkers also. Congratulations!

Cordially,

Clay

H. Clay Alexander, M.D.
HCA/jw

Mr. Law,

In this psychiatrist's opinion, Law's guidance offered in *The Beer Drinker's Dream Diet* is a light-hearted, flavorful course that can be toning for both body and soul.

Sincerely,

Harry B. Woods, M.D.

IVAN ANKENBRANDT, M.D.
La Jolla, California

Congratulations, Mr. Law!

Your book, with methods so easy to follow, makes dieting and exercise great fun for a change.

Ivan Ankenbrandt, M.D.

ROBERT W. INBODY
Senior Vice President, Southern California Region

Dear Elwin:

Let me express my appreciation for taking the time to share your diet with me. It's obvious it's been successful for you and I can tell it will be just as rewarding to me. I'm already within 5 pounds of where I want to be, having already lost 11 pounds.

There is definitely something to the visualization of how you want to look, as I honestly feel confident changing my appearance. I also enjoy being able to drink beer whenever I feel like it without worrying about "blowing my diet."

This is the most sensible, easy-to-follow program for a busy executive to follow as I can do the stomach exercises while I work and never feel pressured to make time for an exercise program.

Best of luck with your book and thanks again for sharing your idea.

Best wishes,

Robert W. Inbody
RWI: slr

San Diego, CA

Dear Elwin,

Talk about skeptical! It couldn't be that easy. There wasn't a diet that I hadn't tried and working as an administrator in a variety of hospital and clinic settings exposed me to most nutritional programs ("diets") that are not made available to the public. Nothing worked. I only had about fifteen pounds to lose and could literally stop eating (which I did during a four-day "cleansing" fast) and not lose a pound.

I couldn't believe it when I decided to "commit" to your program. I lost five pounds in three days!! During the next seven days I lost five more pounds. Total: ten pounds in a week and a half! I believe in the rubber shorts. I wore them under my warm-up suit while playing tennis and the pounds and inches literally melted away.

We've started to use the program with my son who is in a wheelchair. He can't get much exercise due to the severity of his injury at this time, but he can follow your diet. I think the disabled could benefit immensely from *The Beer Drinker's Dream Diet*.

Incidently, I've given up wine which I used to love and now enjoy beer in a champagne glass. It tastes great and is better for me. Thanks!!

Patty Cady

LJ Financial Insurance
Services Corporation

The Beer Drinkers Dream Diet was one of the easiest
and healthiest weight loss programs I've ever been
on. I lost approximately 20 lbs. in four weeks.

Perhaps, most importantly, I have <u>maintained</u> this
weight loss.

Chris L. Jones

Dear Elwin,

My self-esteem had reached a very sensitive point in negotiations with my fat. I was ready to do something to lose weight, but it couldn't be much. I certainly was not prepared to feel deprived in any way. As anyone who is overweight knows, deprivation is not a negotiable point.

I know, or at least suspected, the basic concepts of dieting; eat less, eat smart, exercise. Still, I needed my hand held. I needed to be led. Enter Elwin Law and his new diet book, "*The Beer Drinker's Dream Diet*."

Now, I do not consider myself a chronic beer drinker, but after seeing Elwin following a few months lapse, I was ready to tip a few brews. He looked great! At least thirty pounds thinner than I remembered.

Elwin gave me a copy of his new book and encouraged me to read it. I have indeed read it. I have also followed it, and here is what his diet plan has done for me. In less than a month I slipped from 182 pounds (on a 5'8" frame) to 167 pounds. And I feel great, light and full of energy. I also feel confident that the weight I have lost is gone. G-O-N-E. And I'm not through yet!

If Elwin's diet had made me feel deprived in any way, I wouldn't have stayed on it for a minute. Fortunately, he encouraged me to diet in a uniquely personal writing style that made me feel as though I had a friend dieting right along with me.

I encourage anyone who is almost ready to get serious about their fat to read Elwin Law's *"The Beer Drinker's Dream Diet."* And not just beer drinkers. Beer, you see, only symbolizes anything we eat in excess. I wonder if Elwin planned that?

Rudy Garcia

WHOLESALE JEWELERS, Inc.

Mr. Elwin Law

Dear Elwin:

Being a tennis player and beer devotee, I thought that as the years went on I would be forced to give up one or the other — the little pot belly I had developed wasn't conducive to movement on the tennis court.

I had tried lots of diets . . . They all worked, temporarily.

Thank you so much for sharing your simplistic method of weight reduction (more importantly, control).

I followed it the last four months and have taken off 9 lbs. and kept them off! I love it!

Sincerely,

Rowan K. Klein

GREAT AMERICAN BLDG. · SUITE 1140 · SAN DIEGO, CA 92101 · (619) 234-4429

Dear Reader,

Recently, I set aside a four week period to lose ten pounds. With a five foot, nine inch frame, I am able to carry a little extra weight. However, I am an aspiring tennis professional and I felt that the excess weight was slowing me down.

Thus, I followed the guidelines outlined in Elwin Law's book, *The Beer Drinkers Dream Diet*, for a period of five weeks. I was amazed at how simply the weight came off, how much better I felt, and how easy the program made it to maintain my newly acquired weight.

I've come to the conclusion that anyone with a will to lose weight can do so in a sensible manner. By reading and practicing *The Beer Drinkers Dream Diet*, one does not have to revert to extreme measures to find a desirable weight. This book simplifies the often painful process of weight reduction into a systematic, healthy, and satisfying menu for daily living.

Colleen Clery

San Diego Tennis & Racquet Club

* Throughout the entire 5-week period, I continued to consume an average of 2-3 beers per day.

A Brief History
of Beer

Wouldn't you know it: Women first introduced us to the delectable taste of "liquid bread" several thousand years ago. Members of the fairer sex were the principal brewers back then, and those who brewed beer for the temple ceremonies in Egypt were revered as priestesses. (Sorry about that, Brewmeisters!) They knew what they were doing, too, even by modern standards.

They learned to prepare malt from barley, and they developed strains of yeast for fermentation. During the early Middle Ages, beer making was common to nearly every household and was performed, naturally, by women. (Tell me that drinking beer is *only* for men!)

It is believed that beer was first discovered quite by accident when an infusion of water and mashed grain accidentally came into contact with minute yeast cells. The yeast thereby caused a dramatic change in the liquid, which no doubt startled and fascinated the people at that time. This process, which we call fermentation, transformed some of the sugars in the grains into ethyl alcohol and carbon dioxide, thus producing the intoxicating and bubbly characteristics of beer.

Babylonian tablets over 6,000 years old give detailed recipes for the brewing of beer. Legend has it that Isis, the "mother" of the gods, introduced beer to Egypt, where it was known as *hequp* (no pun intended), and it became the most popular beverage of all the people. Rameses III offered up 30,000 gallons of beer to the gods each year in hopes of quenching their thirst.

The Egyptians believed that a person's love of worldly things would continue after death. As a result, beer was specifically included in many burial offerings to help sustain the dead on their long journey forward or upward or wherever.

Beer has also been found in more than a hundred Egyptian medicinal prescriptions.

Scholars tell us that brewing was not perfected in any one place, but rather was developed among agricultural people scattered across the globe, with each culture having its own particular interest in and special attachment to beer. The Chinese believed that brewing beer was decreed from heaven. To the Saxons, it was a cure for hiccups. Some cultures used beer to induce relaxation . . . others used beer as part of a recipe for leavening bread.

Beer went hand in hand with the spread of civilization throughout Europe. The Britons, Scots and Picts all served it at their feasts and celebrations. It is said that the hearty Vikings ate six meals a day and drank a soup which was made of bread and beer with each of these meals. They also consumed beer from horns before battles, and later at victory celebrations and sexual marathons. Therefore, it was not surprising that when the Vikings descended upon England in the Eighth Century, brewing was one craft that they brought with them.

Beer was a required ration on most ships that touched port in the years of the discovery of the Americas and was considered a protection from malnutrition. When the Pilgrims landed the Mayflower at Plymouth Rock, one of the Pilgrims wrote in his diary that instead of continuing on to Virginia, which was their original plan, "We could not now take time for further search or consideration, our victuals being much spent, especially our beer."

Another one of the travelers to the New World on the Mayflower was John Alden, of the well-known Priscilla Mullins/-Miles Standish "Speak for yourself, John" story. He had come along as cooper to care for the beer barrels.

The first commercial brewery in America was founded in New Amsterdam, which is now New York, in 1623. Director-General Peter Stuyvesant was one of the early regulators of this young New World industry. The pioneers of the industry in the United States included many patriots who owned their own breweries: among them were Samuel Adams and William Penn. George Washington had his own personal recipe for the beer that was brewed at Mount Vernon, his Virginia estate. His handwritten recipe is still preserved.

And did you know that the romantic word "bridal" was derived from "bride ale," which was the name given to old-time English wedding feasts at which ale, naturally, was the featured beverage?

So, you see, beer not only has had a most respectable history, but it has been part of a downright "religious experience" in some instances. Now, who in their right mind would purposely set out on a diet that would mandate giving up this delectable drink? As I said before, I not only didn't give up beer, I didn't even cut down on it. And I assure you, I lost the *weight* and the *inches*!

Before the Diet

What You May Expect From The Beer Drinker's Dream Diet:

1. If you are serious and truly desirous of losing weight and getting into good shape, you can expect to lose between 8 and 30 pounds in one to ten weeks.

2. YOU will be in control, so YOU must be your own monitor. There are not a lot of do's and don'ts in this diet.

3. You should *like* this diet and actually find it *fun* — two important elements in anything you do.

4. You can expect to reward yourself each day — that's right, *reward* yourself — whether with a candle-lit evening meal

including beer, cocktails, or wine, or with some other personal form of "reward," within reasonable limits.

5. Don't expect to suffer or feel deprived because of this diet. On the other hand, remember that what you have done (or not done) in the past has contributed to the shape you are presently in. So do expect to *change* and *challenge* old habits, and *think* about what you do and why you do it.

6. Perhaps one of the most important benefits you can expect to achieve will be the ease at which you MAINTAIN your weight loss. Did you know that approximately 90% of dieters regain their weight after going off their particular diet? Not so with this program.

This is a change of style, of habits, of health awareness, and actually of desires. Remember, you are not really prohibited from doing anything, it's just that after a short time the idea of over-eating or overindulging has very little appeal! Believe me, I know — I've been there, as have others who have been on this diet.

One of the things that I used to really enjoy was having an early breakfast at the LaValencia Hotel in La Jolla, comprising a large steak, two eggs over easy, juice, coffee, two glasses of milk, and an English muffin with butter and jam. I thoroughly enjoyed every mouthful. Naturally, I was more than just a little full afterwards!

Now after being on *The Beer Drinker's Dream Diet*, I have no desire to overeat like that. The idea of all that food for breakfast has become a bit repulsive. I could do it if I wanted to, and I could adjust the amount I eat for lunch and dinner so I probably wouldn't gain any

weight, but the idea of eating that
much is just not appealing. I might
take that same meal and cut it in half
— that's much more appealing.

Besides my stomach feels like it has
"shrunk," as yours will, even though
that doesn't really happen. You will just
find that your appetite will adjust ac-
cordingly.

But one of the greatest benefits of this
program will be the natural ease with
which you maintain the weight you will
have so beautifully lost.

Since I got down to my goal of 175
pounds, I have fluctuated perhaps 3 or
4 pounds above and below that weight.
By weighing yourself every day, you too
will be able to adjust your intake imme-
diately if you should need to.

7. You may expect this diet to be easy —
in fact, too easy! The principles contained in this book are so simple that
you may worry — if it doesn't hurt, and
if it's not terribly demanding, something must be wrong!

However, quite the opposite is true:
some of the finest achievements have
been accomplished with tremendous
ease.

When you are really in tune with yourself and your goals, your efforts often
appear effortless! Such is the case with
this diet.

You Will Lose Weight Beautifully!

H ave you ever noticed that most "diet books" are big and fat, with umpteen-hundred pages stuck between the covers? Well, this book is slim and sleek. It's a short book because when a theory works, it doesn't take a lot of space to get the idea across. We don't need a lot of pages and excess bulk to accomplish our objective.

This is a diet book with all the fat trimmed off! More is not necessarily better. This applies both to the number of pages in a book and to the amount of food one eats.

This book is a no-nonsense program without a lot of frills, one that focuses on the bottom line — loss of weight and inches — without leaving you feeling deprived.

Each year millions of dollars are spent on diets, health clubs, group sessions, hypnosis, etc., in a sincere effort by very well-meaning people to lose weight and get into better physical shape. Some are successful, many are not, and the "success" is often for only a brief period of time.

There have been countless books written on *dieting* and how to lose weight: calorie counters, carbohydrate counters, juicers, grapefruits, "eating lists" for Tuesdays and an entirely different one for Wednesdays, ad infinitum. Not that these books don't have their place, but their approaches were not for me, and what I have written here is not an attempt to add to that list.

Numerous books also have been written on *exercise,* even going so far as to promise you weight loss. But even though exercise is indeed very beneficial, exercise alone will not do the trick. My answer lies in the *special combination* of six principles that you will find uniquely put together in *The Beer Drinker's Dream Diet.*

Questions Most Frequently Asked About The Beer Drinker's Dream Diet:

Question: Is this another fad diet book? I'm so tired of them.

Answer: Thank you for that wonderful question. I think the whole world is tired of the fad diet books that go to such extremes for the temporary loss of a few pounds, to say nothing of their questionable nutritional value.

This is anything but a fad diet book. It is a *fun* diet book and a way of life as you will see. Behavior is modified to a certain extent, and you will begin to start thinking about yourself and what you eat. You'll love the changes in you and your life.

Question: I'm a big guy and I enjoy my beer, sometimes more on those block-bustering, sports-filled weekends. I'd like to drop a few pounds but I don't want to give up my beer. Any hope?

Answer: You, friend, are exactly who this book is for. Read it. Follow the plan, and you can already give me a "high five" for the results!

Question: Do I have to drink beer for this diet to work?

Answer: No, you don't have to drink beer for this diet to work for you with amazing results. It will work *even though* you drink beer — a lot of it!

Question: I don't drink beer, but I do have a problem with sweets and pasta, if you know what I mean. Will this diet work for me?

Answer: Absolutely, this diet will work for you, no matter what your "problem" foods are. The BEHAVIORAL PRINCIPLES contained in this book are what count.

Question: I'm not really a beer drinker, but am I ever married to one! What will he think of my buying this book for him? My husband really needs to lose some weight.

Answer: He would probably love you for it. It shows you really care about

him and about his looks and
health and that you also care
about his appreciation and enjoyment of his beer. You're not
asking him to give it up.

He will, in fact, have the best of
both worlds, and so will you as
those inches start to drop away.

Go for it!

Now Let's Get Started!

T his program has been divided into mornings, afternoons, and evenings, indicating the rules to be followed during each period.

Some of the things that I will ask you to do may seem quite trivial, but DO THEM! *They are important!*

Every statement has a reason and purpose and should be followed.

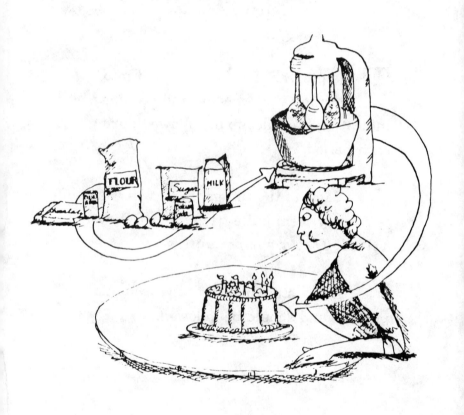

Analogy of a Cake

The Analogy
of a Cake —
A Recipe for Life

N ow I'm going to share with you the
actual things I did while losing 27
pounds and removing 6 inches from my
waist.

First, let's consider a very simple
analogy. (As simple as it is, it is absolutely
essential to this book and will give you the
wonderful results you want.)

A person setting out to make a cake
usually has a specific recipe that calls for
perhaps six or eight basic ingredients.

Each item alone accomplishes nothing: it's when they're mixed together and
blended in their proper combination that the
result is a magnificent cake!

If even just one item is left out, say sugar, there's no way the cake is going to come out right.

This same principle applies to the elements and ingredients of *The Beer Drinker's Dream Diet* — it's the **combination** of all of them that will bring the desired results.

Although it sounds incredibly (maybe too) easy, it's absolutely essential to include all the ingredients of the program if you want to maximize the benefits.

Mornings

1. EVERY MORNING —
   UPON AWAKENING VISUALIZE THE
   WEIGHT LOSS YOU WANT:
   TRIMMER WITHOUT THAT EXTRA
   POUNDAGE.

   See yourself in a bathing suit at the beach, in tennis shorts or in beautifully tailored clothes at a party. No matter how far away you may presently be from that ideal, continue picturing and visualizing this. Visualization should not take more than two minutes.

   It may help to look at a snapshot of a trimmer you to get the picture in your mind.

   VISUALIZE your scale, and imagine the needle pointing to the number of pounds you want to weigh. I would suggest starting off with 5 pound increments of weight loss.

Visualize

For example, if you weigh 200 pounds and want to drop to 180 pounds, visualize 195 on the scale first. I mean really SEE it! Let it burn into your mind, until you have a permanent image that you can recall at any time of the day. When you have achieved that, go to 190, etc.

Once that special thing called momentum starts to work for you, it will automatically tend to perpetuate itself and build, making weight loss easier and easier.

Studies have shown that if you are able to visualize yourself being thinner in the future, you will lose weight faster and more permanently.[1] *Do yourself a favor and let your mind help you lose weight!*

---

[1]Olness, K. et al. Group hypnotherapy in the management of obesity. Presented at American Society of Clinical Hypnosis, New Orleans, 1971.

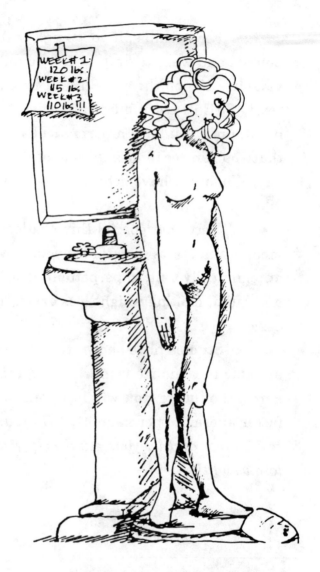

Weigh Yourself Every Morning

2. WEIGH YOURSELF EVERY MORNING BEFORE BREAKFAST.

Checking your weight every morning is essential. That's the only way of honestly keeping track.

Momentum and results will begin to accelerate as you begin to notice that little needle on the scale drop first one, two, then more and more pounds!

3. PERFORM FIVE MINUTES OF EASY
    MORNING EXERCISE.

Before eating or drinking anything, do a few of the following simple
exercises. Don't make them strenuous or
laborious; you are simply waking up and
starting the blood circulating.

- STRETCH those arms, legs, and torso
  in all directions, slowly and smoothly,
  much the way a cat stretches and
  flexes.

- STOMACH PULL-INS achieve incredible results. It's amazing what can be
  accomplished from this simple exercise — *It's perhaps the most important exercise you'll be doing.* This
  exercise is a form of yoga — dynamic
  tension-in-reverse.

  Bend over with hands on knees and
  exhale all air. Pull your stomach *in*

and *up* toward your chest and *hold* it for three to five seconds. Repeat eight times. It's so easy but *do* it! The results will be fantastic. Visualize the toning and strengthening of the stomach muscles as you do this exercise.

Stomach pull-ins should be done throughout the day, while sitting at your desk, driving, standing, etc. (You don't have to bend over with hands on knees during these times.) This exercise is wonderful for muscle toning and waist reduction.

To repeat: *This is one of the most important exercises you will be doing!*

Stomach Pull-ins

- Do any OTHER EXERCISES — SIT-UPS, LEG RAISES or PUSH-UPS — you want, all at your own speed but really get the blood circulating! Total time of these easy morning exercises should be *no more than five minutes*!

Be sure that you don't con yourself into thinking that you simply can't spare that amount of time. YOU KNOW YOU CAN! This is one of the habits you may well be changing.

Another little secret — after these five minutes of exercise, you will feel refreshed and really awake!

On all counts, YOU WIN!

4. EAT WHAT YOU WANT FOR BREAK-
FAST, BUT CUT ALL PORTIONS IN
HALF!

That's right, CUT THEM IN
HALF! If you are used to two eggs and a
piece of toast, have only one egg and
half a piece of toast. Have a half-glass of
orange juice rather than a full glass.
Same with your cereal. (These half portions will be only for breakfast and
lunch.)

Be acutely aware that this principle of cutting the portions in half is ex-
tremely important! I can hear you say-
ing, "Ouch, I can't do that!" Really, you
CAN do it and with total ease. I'll tell
you why.

Cut Portions in Half

After 15 Minutes Hunger is Gone

The Myth of Feeling Full

T his is perhaps the most important discovery I have made. Many of us have
been taught since childhood to eat until we
felt full (or, in more genteel terms "have had
a sufficiency"). So we continued to eat until
we were full — or more accurately, stuffed!

And now, here I am telling you to cut
your portions in half! "Ridiculous!" you say.
But wait a minute. The great thing I discovered is that although yes, you probably *will*
still be hungry after the last little crumb
from that meager half portion is gone from
your plate, stop eating anyway!

*Because within fifteen to twenty min-
utes your hunger will be gone!*

That's right. GONE! And as the days go by, it won't even take fifteen minutes. In fact, as you become thinner, your hunger will turn off sooner and sooner.

In addition, your energy level will increase. It may take a little adjustment at first, but *it works*!

The following is what Herb Boynton, past president of a leading nutrition company, has to say on the matter:

"Yes, it is true that your appetite will turn off in fifteen to twenty minutes, even if you eat half of what you usually do.

Why should this be so? After a meal is consumed, several mechanisms combine to produce satiety — to tell you that you're not hungry any more.

These mechanisms include distention of the stomach and upper intestines to allow a feeling of fullness, and also the release of certain intestinal hormones.

However, probably the most important mechanism is the increase in blood sugar that rises to optimal levels about fifteen to twenty minutes after eating. This increase signals the brain that your blood sugar is now at a satisfactory level, and there isn't any further need to eat.

In effect, your body tells your brain that you're no longer hungry. This happens even if you eat much less than you are accustomed to."[2]

---

[2]Powers, P. *Obesity: The regulation of weight.* Baltimore, 1980, pp.

Carbohydrates: Secret Helper #1

This is the only time that I am going to specifically talk about what kinds of foods to eat on *The Beer Drinker's Dream Diet*. What I have found is very important to share with you — not only for energy and nutritional purposes — but also for greater speed and ease in losing weight.

You must have an open mind and be willing to challenge old beliefs.

What are carbohydrates? There are two basic types: *simple carbohydrates* (sugars), such as are found in cookies, cakes, soft drinks, and ice creams; and *complex carbohydrates* (starches) found in breads, rice and other grains, pasta and some vegetables.

Carbohydrates, not proteins, are the body's main source of energy. This is one reason that so many people on low-carbohydrates become irritable, depressed, and weak — they aren't getting much energy! They soon fall off their diet with a strong feeling of deprivation and a sense of failure.

Studies have shown that a person on a diet containing adequate carbohydrates should feel energetic, alert, and basically optimistic. Obviously, when you feel good you are able to stick to something much more easily. Remember, *carbohydrates are your main source of energy!*

Eating a high carbohydrate, low-fat diet generates more body heat and burns off more calories than eating a low-carbohydrate diet. Your metabolism runs at a higher level when fueled with a high proportion of carbohydrates.

All those calories from carbohydrates go mainly toward increasing glycogen (muscle fuel) *without* causing an increase in body fat.[3]

---

[3]Dept. of Health, Education and Welfare, National Institute of Health. *Obesity in America*. NIH Publication No. 79.359. Nov. 1979, p. 57.

Carbohydrates also decrease hunger pangs and give you that full feeling when you've finished your meal. In one study, a group of overweight men went on a strict diet which cut their calories in half but also included a large proportion of carbohydrates.

Despite the marked reduction in food intake and a dramatic loss of weight; they rarely experienced hunger sensations. Why not?

High-carbohydrate diets maintain blood glucose at normal levels over a prolonged period of time. This may be why people on a high-carbohydrate diet rarely complain of hunger.[4]

---

[4]Mickleson, O., et al. Weight Loss With a Reduced Calorie High Fiber Bread. Am. Jrn. of Clinical Nutrition, pp. 1703. 1979.

Fiber:
Secret Helper #2

W hen high-fiber foods are eaten, they quickly absorb water and expand. This causes the stomach and intestines to distend, and this signals "fullness" to the brain even before your blood sugar level has risen.

For this and other reasons, high-fiber foods are certainly to be recommended in any weight-reduction regimen.

Although wheat bran is the best-known source of fiber, whole grains and most unrefined fruits and vegetables are also good sources.[5]

Studies have shown that people on a high-fiber, low-protein diet lose more weight than those on a high-protein, low-fiber diet.

---

[5]Mickelson, O., et al. Prevention and treatment of obesity. In Schemmel, R., ed. *Nutrition, physiology and obesity.* Boca Raton, CRC Press, 1980.

Foods containing high amounts of fiber (fresh fruits, vegetables and whole grains) directly combat and "neutralize" much of your calorie intake.

Combining high-fiber foods with other foods will neutralize much of the calorie intake by preventing the absorption of many calories.[6]

To apply this to everyday living, be sure to include salads and whole grains in your daily meals. They are so easy, so good, and filled with nutrition!

---

[6]Heaton, K.W. Food fiber as an obstacle to energy intake. *Lancet*, 2. 1973. p. 1918.

Afternoons

1. FOR LUNCH, again eat what you want, but CUT ALL PORTIONS IN HALF.

The same principles apply here as for breakfast. I don't want to talk calories — I want to keep things simple. As a demonstration, let's see what cutting my portions in half at lunch did for my calorie intake.

First, a fact: *To lose one pound, you must burn 3,500 more calories than you take in.* That means in order to lose one pound per week, you must decrease your "caloric balance" by 500 calories a day (3,500 calories divided by 7 days).

Now let's take a look at my typical lunch before *The Beer Drinker's Dream Diet*:

Club sandwich (bacon, chicken, tomato, three pieces of bread, mayonnaise, lettuce)	690 calories
Corn chips, one bag	240 calories
Soft drink, one 8-ounce glass	105 calories
	1035 calories

Cutting this typical lunch in half would save me over 500 calories — one lunch alone! Making *just this one change, and no other,* would cause me to lose one pound a week!

And remember, any hunger you feel right after your meal will be gone in just twenty minutes. Test it out for yourself — you'll be delighted at this discovery.

2. DO PULL-IN STOMACH EXERCISES.

Don't forget to do these vitally important exercises thirty to forty times, throughout the day. They are so easy and simple to
do, and the results will be great.

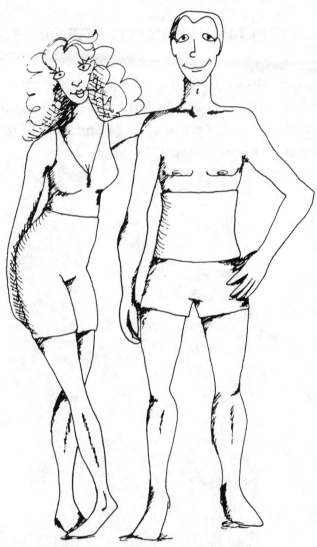

**Exercise with Rubber Belt or
Rubber Shorts**

3. EXERCISE WITH RUBBER WAIST BELT OR RUBBER SHORTS.

"You've got to be kidding," you say! But it's no joke, they work! In combination with all the other principles of *The Beer Drinker's Dream Diet*, they will work miracles.

Remember the cake analogy? You've got to combine all the ingredients — don't leave out the sugar! To be sure, this is one of those unique ingredients, but wearing the rubber belt or shorts is an important part of this total program. Laugh, snicker, but DO IT!

I want to encourage you to really "go for it" during these exercises. Recall how all the beer commercials stress that it's always after a hard, sweaty game or job that one looks forward to that cool, rich beer. Besides, it's great for your health. So put a little gut into your workout!

Disregard what you may have previously heard about rubber exercise clothes.

They absolutely **do** work if used as part of this total program. They worked for me, so why not for you? Use them in the following manner:

- Put them on and do eight stomach pull-ins.

- Do 50 to 100 side bends.

- Then, with the belt or shorts on under your clothes, enjoy your favorite sport — tennis, jogging, walking, bicycling, aerobics, weight-lifting, even gardening.

  Be sure to leave the belt or shorts on for at least thirty minutes after finishing your exercises.

If you are one of those people who do not do any of these active sports, or if you do not have time that particular day, then make up some exercises right in the privacy of your own home. Concentrate on the *body areas* where you want most to reduce. Do them to music or while watching TV, doing housework, etc., so that exercise becomes a routine part of your day.

Be sure to fit this exercise in sometime during your day. *Remember* — the *more* exercise you do, the *less* hungry you will be. It sounds strange, but I've found that exercise takes my appetite away.

I cannot emphasize too strongly the importance of the *psychological value* and momentum established in actually seeing the inches melt away when you take off your belt or shorts, and that wonderful feeling of being just a bit lighter and smaller in the right areas.

After you get down to the proper weight and size, you won't have to use the belt or shorts every day, but they are actually kind of fun, as well as providing support for your back.

Here is what Herb Boynton has to say about the rubber belt and rubber shorts:

"The use of rubber shorts while exercising can dramatically reduce the size of waist, hips, and thighs, literally in a few hours, simply by diverting water from these tissues.

This effect is usually temporary because water will return to these tissues within a few days. However, by combining exercise and diet, fatty tissue is removed from the waist, hips, and thighs, as well as water.

Thus, the effect becomes gratifyingly permanent."

Evenings

1. REWARD YOURSELF — YOU DESERVE IT!

In the late afternoon, or after dinner, relax and enjoy a beer or two, or any other drink of your choice. If from 7 a.m. to 5 p.m. you keep in mind the rules of the diet, then you will have an evening of relaxation and enjoyment to look forward to.

How civilized dieting can be! It's not really dieting at all.

IT'S A PROGRAM FOR LIVING.

There have been many people on this diet who drank six or more beers a day and still achieved great results with loss of weight and inches. Others prefer just one or two drinks.

It obviously depends on individual preference as well as on physiological make-up; each one of us is different.

Beer makes a wonderful snack because it is:

- low in calories: a 12-ounce beer has only 140 calories. That's less than the equivalent amount of wine.

- nutritious: beer is rich in B vitamins, including niacin. It is low in sugar and high in complex carbohydrates.[7]

- relaxing: beer relieves tension as well as hunger.

- filling: all those natural carbon dioxide bubbles give your stomach an immediate feeling of fullness. Soon afterward, the carbohydrates in beer work to decrease your hunger pangs.

---

[7]Gaslineau et al. *Fermented food: Beverages in nutrition.* New York: Academic Press, 1979.

Reward Yourself

A drink may have a positive effect on your life span and cardiovascular health.

A study done at a major university found that moderate beer drinkers may have a smaller risk for heart attack than both teetotalers and occasional drinkers.[8]

---

[8]Richman, A. Cardiovascular disease in moderate drinkers. *Drug and Alcohol Dependence Journal*, 1985.

2. ENJOY YOUR EVENING MEAL!

It's time for a great dinner — your choice of foods *and* full portions if you choose! Live it up! Try for a meal that includes a serving of starch, has a low-fat protein source such as chicken or fish, and includes a fiber-rich food such as a fresh salad, whole grains, or vegetables.

If you can bring yourself to reduce the portions at the evening meal, so much the better. Try to eat this meal several hours before you go to sleep.

If you prefer to have your main meal at lunchtime, follow these instructions and cut your *evening meal* in half.

Enjoy!

3. BEFORE YOU GO TO SLEEP, VISUALIZE THE WEIGHT LOSS YOU WANT.

See yourself in your mind the way you want to be. See the desired weight on the scales. See the slender look you desire.

This visualization exercise should take no more than two minutes.

Interesting data from a prominent nutrition company in California:

HIDDEN FAT

"Do you know that fat contains 2½ times as many calories per ounce as either protein or carbohydrates? Fat is calorie dense, so be sure to limit your intake. Most people don't, however. The *average American* gets a whopping 42.5% of total calories from fat — 20 to 30% is a reasonable figure.

Here's a list of foods that supply *over* 50% of their calories from fat — and I'll bet you thought most of them were high protein foods:

wieners and frankfurters	up to 80%
peanuts and peanut butter	almost 70%
most cheeses	up to 75%
most lunch meats	up to 80%
eggs	65%, more if fried
ground beef - regular	up to 75%
bacon	up to 80%
pork	up to 75%
granola	up to 53%
filet mignon	up to 80%

Even milk (whole milk) is 48% fat in terms of calorie content. *Look for the hidden fat in your diet* and get rid of it. This also means that you must go easy on butter, margarine, tartar sauce, and salad dressings which are almost 100% fat!

The following is a brief discussion of beer by Mr. Boynton:

NUTRIENT CONTENT OF BEER

"Beer and beer-like beverages have been consumed since prehistoric times. They are brewed from a mixture of rice, barley, and small amounts of hops which are acted upon by brewer's yeast in a fermentation process which produces beer including small amounts of alcohol.

Rice and barley are nutritious grains, and a good deal of the nutrient content of the grains is transferred to the beer.

Beer typically contains some B-complex vitamins, a number of minerals and important trace elements including magne-

sium and significant amounts of the important trace element chromium. Chromium
works with the hormone insulin to normal-
ize blood sugar levels and is thus an important factor in the production of biological
energy.

Beer, the beverage of moderation, is
also surprisingly nutritious.

The Six Rules of The Beer Drinker's Dream Diet

1. VISUALIZE the weight loss you want
    twice a day, upon waking and before
    sleeping.

2. WEIGH YOURSELF before breakfast
    every day.

3. DO FIVE MINUTES OF EXERCISE
    three times a day; before breakfast,
    lunch, and dinner. (Do include a more
    strenuous afternoon exercise, definitely
    using the rubber weight belt or shorts.)

4. CUT YOUR BREAKFAST AND LUNCH
    IN HALF. TWENTY MINUTES AFTER
    EATING YOU WILL FEEL COM-
    PLETELY SATISFIED.

5. CHOOSE HIGH-CARBOHYDRATE, LOW-FAT, AND HIGH-FIBER FOODS.

6. REWARD YOURSELF! Relax and enjoy a beer or other beverage in the afternoon or early evening.

Each rule is simple in and of itself, but it's the combination of the rules that gives you the wonderful results you want.

Although these rules are incredibly easy, it's absolutely essential to follow them all to maximize the benefits.

Tips and Reminders

1. Choose your foods carefully:

    -   Low-fat protein sources, such as fish and chicken
    -   Low-fat dairy products
    -   Starches in moderate amounts: pasta, rice, potatoes
    -   High-fiber foods: whole grains, bran, raw vegetables and fruits

2. Cut back on problem foods:

    -   Red meats and prepared meats (hot dogs, bologna, etc.)
    -   Salt, and foods with high sodium content
    -   Sauteed and fried foods
    -   Creamy salad dressings
    -   Sweets
    -   Oil, and high-fat foods such as cheeses, butter, margarine, cream

3.   Eat slowly. The more times you chew, the sooner your hunger will be satisfied.

4.   Be conscious of what you are eating. Take the time to taste and enjoy your food.

5.   Be patient. Hunger will pass within fifteen to twenty minutes after you finish eating. And don't just sit around thinking about food. GET BUSY DOING SOMETHING ELSE.

     The less you eat, the less you will want. Soon the idea of overeating and having that stuffed feeling will become repugnant to you.

6.   Help yourself. Don't keep your particular "problem foods" in the house. If there aren't any of them around, you'll be less tempted.

7. Start a new habit. Once momentum is established in a particular direction, it tends to perpetuate itself. Get momentum going in the right direction. We are creatures of habit, and habits can be changed.

8. Take a good vitamin and mineral supplement daily.

9. Do not get discouraged. If your diet partner is losing weight faster than you are, don't worry. Women, for instance, naturally have more fatty tissue than men, so it normally takes a woman somewhat longer to lose weight, but you *will* achieve your goal!

10. DO NOT DRINK AND DRIVE! If you wish to enjoy drinking in moderation or in the privacy of your own home, that's great.

After the Diet

THE END

That's it, my friend — short, simple, and to the point! Have *fun* and *enjoy* it, all the way to the tailor!

One other thing — Share ***The Beer Drinker's Dream Diet*** with a friend.

And, last but not least: "Cheers!"